# GOOD LUCK,

# BAD LUCK,

# OR NO LUCK?

## By Gregory Heary

One troubling trend amongst people today is the belief in "Luck". If you ask "What is Luck?" giving the impression you never heard of it before they are at a loss of words to explain what exactly "Luck" is. They've never actually thought about it but just believed that it existed. First we must know what luck is before we can come to classify it, if it exists.

In America number 7 is considered to be lucky. Despite there being 13 original states and 13 stripes on the American flag, many Americans consider the number 13 to be unlucky. Some historians may come up with various excuses for why those numbers in particular were deemed influential but in reality they are just numbers. Also Jesus pbuh is widely believed to have had 12 disciples, so as a group: 1 Jesus pbuh + 12 disciples = 13. But it would be blasphemy to consider Jesus pbuh and his disciples unlucky. Ironically in China people consider the number 13 to be lucky and the number 7 to be unlucky. To this day neither Americans nor Chinese have produced solid evidences to support their numerical inclinations and aversions which are coincidentally directly opposite of each other. How is it possible that the same number can be considered lucky to one people and unlucky to another people? The same number cannot possibly be both lucky and unlucky. This means "Luck" is solely a matter of perspective, subject to be interpreted any way one wants. None of these interpretations are based on sound judgment or reasoning but "Luck" is just used as a scapegoat. A winner never credits "luck" as being the cause, it is always their opponents and the losers who say "*they're just lucky*" because they don't want to admit defeat or having lost without supernatural forces being aligned against them. Instead of admitting their own miscalculations or inferiority the losers place the blame on "bad luck" instead of themselves or the superiority of others. It's easier to blame "luck" than skill because "luck" is a four letter word.

No instruments are available to determine the quantity or quality of luck one has. Thus there is no proof for the existence in luck. To believe in "Luck" of any kind is to say that there is no such thing as pre-ordained destiny or that God has no control over what happens and that "Luck" has some power over you either for or against. We often don't think about it but when we say "good luck" we are essentially saying God can't help you, and you need "luck" of the good kind in order to achieve success. In reality if God doesn't want your success, or wants a different outcome, then what

God desires is going to happen. Luck has essentially become a god who we believe has control over our affairs. This makes us deny responsibility and instead of blaming ourselves or just accepting what God has decreed patiently with gratitude, we unjustly involve luck. Some even go to the extremes of having "Lucky charms" such as a horse's shoe or a rabbit's foot. How lucky can a rabbit's foot be if the rabbit no longer has it attached to their body? If a human loses a foot, we call them a cripple, we don't say that's a lucky human foot. When we see these charms for what they are we see how ridiculous believing in them is. In our society these "lucky" tokens have become idols some of which are treated as sacred or powerful. But why would someone ever sell an object if it were really "lucky"? If it were actually lucky wouldn't they make more money by using the charm themselves gambling? The real reason "lucky" charms are sold is because they are useless.

Usually luck is most frequently mentioned when gambling, which we shouldn't be doing anyways. Nevertheless gambling experiences tend to be the setting when people are first introduced to the concept of "luck". Gambling is a whole different topic, but at the bare bones gambling is a tax on stupid people who cannot understand math, that have vast misconceptions about probability. If you flip a fair coin there is a 50% probability it will land on a certain side, in a ratio 1:2. However if you flip it 2 times the probability is still 1:2 and the coin doesn't take into account what side it landed on the first time or how many times it has been flipped. Likewise if you flip it 20 times and it lands on the same side every time that does not mean the 21st time is any more likely to land on the different side than when you flipped it initially. Every time the probability is the same, the odds do not get better with time or change, they constantly remain exactly the same. 50% probability is 50% whether it's the first time or the 100th. This is known as the gambler's fallacy in which the gambler thinks past results influences future outcomes making them more probable and therefore potentially exploitable for prediction, so they put money on the prediction and take a gamble hoping to be right. But the odds are still the same and they have no better chance than at any other time during the game. This has been proven to gamblers many times over with heavy financial losses resulting, but because of their belief in "luck" they think the rules of the world do not apply to them, because they think they are more lucky than the rest or that some lucky idol they possess will make the outcome favorable for them. While neurologically the pathological gambler's brain interprets a "near win" as a win and it causes the same happy feeling in their brains even though it's a loss. This is why 50% of scratch-off lottery tickets are designed to make the person feel they "nearly won", people think they are randomly created but they are actually designed to make someone think they are "lucky" and that their pattern of "nearly winning" will pay off since they are "so close". Whereas the reason they're "so close" is because 50% of the tickets are "near winning losses". The birthday scratch offs are the worst because they are designed to be played in front of a crowd to lead the audience to tell the gambler they are "lucky", especially when the ticket is designed to pay out a small amount. In fact the practices done at birthday celebrations themselves, such as a party, gift giving and blowing out candles, originate from pagan rituals thought to bring health, wealth, protection and fortune; or as it's called today "luck". With birthdays cultivating arrogance, selfishness, greed, wastefulness, and unjustified feelings of entitlement in order to promote hedonism it is a vital element of modern consumerist societies used to lubricate the economy. The birthday scratch offs are designed to pay out more often than the regular ones but for less than the ticket cost, because the gambler is rarely the one who pays, so the company makes a $5 payout seem like a winner to the gambler even though its a loser because it cost $10 to buy. Thus cultivating the "lucky" feeling of the gambler, especially if they win or "nearly win" every year, while the company profits off their "wins". At the same time it's free advertising to the whole crowd because the one who gifts the birthday scratch off is usually too embarrassed to say that they spent $10 on a $5 gift, so they tell the person they're "lucky" rather than admitting they made a stupid wasteful lazy inconsiderate purchase that is designed to develop destructive financial and spiritual habits. Even the slot machines are programmed to show "near wins" and give small payouts in order to develop this "lucky feeling" in a person that leads to compulsive gambling. Casinos spend billions in advertising towards promoting the idea of luck. Now if luck were real then wouldn't you think casinos would want to keep that a secret? After all they would have much to lose if some lucky people played their games, on the other hand if luck isn't real they have much to gain by getting their marks to believe in luck. Casinos would not exist if they were losing money. So either all casinos and their employees are extremely lucky, or luck doesn't exist and they are just profiting from people's ignorance of probability. Which of the two do you think is more likely? If the casino faculty is lucky then how do they measure the luck of a person when they interview for a job at the casino to see if they are "lucky enough" to work there? Why is the "lucky guy" the favorite client of the bookie? Why do casino employees "*wish you luck*" and advise that you should "*try your luck*"? If luck was real then wishing luck to its visitors would cost the casino money. Rather what casino operators don't say is that they don't really "*wish you luck*" instead they just "*wish you believe in luck*" because it makes them very wealthy. Casinos telling the masses that luck exists has been their most lucrative sales pitch and made many casino owners excessively rich, all at the lucky person's expense.

Luck is a multi-billion dollar industry, from the charms and tokens to the shirts with slogans, along with the "wishing well" fountains. If it was tangible then people would sell luck to suckers by the ton. But because luck is a gambling delusion, no mass produced consumer friendly "luck" has ever been produced because once the gambling community proved it didn't work it would jeopardize the entire industry. Luck is a fraudulent marketing scheme that cashes in on foolish people's hopes and dreams.

Not only is Luck immeasurable but it is unknowable and imperceptible. Despite all of this some will still say they "*feel lucky*", this is just optimism and they cannot describe it any other way except by saying it's a special feeling. This is debilitating towards society because it prevents people from having confidence and developing self-esteem. For example there is a famous expression that usually goes something like this: "*You just got a lucky horseshoe up your butt.*" Now I can't speak from personal experience, but I don't think "lucky" is how I would describe having a metal shoe from a horse's hoof lodged deep inside my rectum. That sounds like it would feel excruciatingly painful, but people say that's called "*being lucky*". Although why is the horseshoe in particular considered lucky in any sense at all? Because ancient pagans used it as a symbol of the female reproductive organ which they worshipped as a fertility object for fortune, health, reproduction and crop harvests. Basically the horseshoe is the modern version of the "yoni" symbol or to be blunt the womb or vagina. While since sinful sex has historically been considered as "magical" or a "lucky experience", to have a "horseshoe up your butt" meant one was so promiscuous they'd even "get lucky" and fall into fornication even by expelling their feces. Being told *"You just got a lucky horseshoe up your butt."* use to mean you were a promiscuous whore and the speaker was jealous calling you a "sex magnet". Other sexual/lucky practices are less easily identifiable as religious. For example males amidst hip-hop culture are known to grab their crotch, typically because of emotion or to stop their pants from falling down; but there is a pagan origin behind it. Italian machismos would grab their penis for "good luck" and ancient pagans would literally worship phallic(penis) idols, for a male version of a fertility deity. So while it's typically not done with conscious motivation as an act of phallic worship, many guys involved in hip-hop culture subconsciously grab their privates for *"good luck"* since phallic idols used to be considered "good luck charms". Personally I can say it doesn't work and if God's prophets didn't grab their crotches, we shouldn't do this either. Such crotch grabbing might even be a sign of sexual addictions. However while you may think I've digressed into "dick talk", the point is that all "lucky charms" are as stupid and as ineffective as grabbing your private parts for power. All of these "lucky ideologies" diverts recognition away from people who deserve acknowledgement while allowing others to avoid blame and accountability when they are culpable.

Luck is a mockery of God that makes Satan laugh when we believe in it or speak of it as though it were real. If luck had any influence on sports athletes would practice improving it, but no coach tells their team to "*get better luck*" or that they need it, because they know luck has no impact on the game whatsoever. Rather fans invent "*unlucky curses*" because they don't want to admit their team sucks. Of course the poorly performing teams encourage their fans to think they have bad luck because even they themselves don't want to face the truth about their abilities. It's bad business for a sports franchise to blame themselves for having a losing tradition. But as soon as they start winning then they drop the charade and take all the credit, they're not going to let "luck" take their glory away. Luck is the sports fans scapegoat so they don't have to feel as embarrassed when cheering for the losing team. But while the curse that never was is lifted and the "unlucky" streak ends, the team that they defeated picks up the unlucky slogan and claims the other team only won "*because they got lucky*". But how could they "*get lucky*" when they never practiced to improve their luck?  Imagine putting in years and years of hard work and effort, training to kick, catch or throw a ball.  Finally an opportunity comes and you perform successfully in the vital moments of a highly publicized game. You sacrificed your life to obtain the ability to gain victory for your team in this rare clutch moment, this is your lifetime accomplishment unlikely to ever happen again; this is the apex of your career when you deserve showers of accolades.  Then millions of people around the world say: *"oh he just got lucky, they didn't deserve to win"*.  Imagine that you spent your whole life working for something that you finally accomplished and then the world tells you briskly that *"you just got lucky"*.  This is what happens to many professional athletes.  But they don't make a big deal out of it because they want to play the luck card when they lose.

The reason a person cannot explain luck is because it is a figment of their imagination.  People only believe in it because someone blamed or credited luck as the cause for something they witnessed.  Although "Luck" had nothing to do with the outcome of whatever it was, the word luck was mentioned to make the individual feel special or cursed.  Frequently "Luck" is taught in order to control a young child's feelings, either sparing them from the sorrowful feelings of inferiority or preventing their confidence from soaring exponentially.

Luck isn't exclusively restricted to children, people of all ages come into contact with this poison. The term poison is appropriate because I've been in hospitals and witnessed "luck" being prescribed as medicine. I nearly lost my patience among the patients observing this type of medical and irreligious deceptive malpractice. There were numerous injured, sick and dying patients with death ever present on their minds. Then a "professional" would tell them they'll get better if they're "lucky", or that they're "lucky" their condition isn't worse. All these injured people were at a potential turning point in their lives, they recognized what was most important to them in life and for the first time some began to try to have a relationship with God and repent. Instead of nurses and doctors encouraging this spirituality, their advice was *cross your fingers and hope for the best*. I doubted that crossing one's fingers would help the body to heal and many had injuries completely unrelated to their hands. Hope could have been useful, but they taught the unhealthy to place their hope in superstition. Instead of stressing therapy they considered luck to be more important. Therefore it was not surprising that the hospital held routine gambling events where the patients were encouraged to "*try their luck*" just as if they were at a casino. Most patients wanted to escape since it was expensive to be "cared for". Instead they were told they'd only be allowed to leave if they were "lucky". It was as though they were not allowed to mention God because it was against hospital regulations. Whereas I would've thought hospitals full of the injured would have some of the most religious people on earth working there. It became clear why this wasn't the case after a couple of days observation. God did not figure into their medical equation of caretaking, the main factor was something called "luck", but I never saw them testing the levels of luck that patients had. When patients were released they would be told "*Bye and Good luck*". I wondered to myself if they say "*Hi and Bad luck*" when the patients first come in. This was the worst possible medicine injured people could have been given. In their time of need when they can potentially change their life and mindset for the better and get on the road to paradise and be grateful for what they have, the patients are subliminally told that God can't help them "*Luck is all you need*". Some hospital staff may also advise hard work and improved health as a requirement for the patients to get released. Although generally whenever staff was asked about how long until the release date, the answer was frequently "*I don't know it depends*" with undertones implying that luck was the deciding factor. Granted I may be writing too deep into this but I saw those unhealthy patients actually become less religious. It would be one thing if hospitals were secular and strictly scientific prohibiting religious activity on their property. But they are neither scientific nor secular and teach their patients to believe in the superstition of "Luck", which is a pagan religion. The person comes into the hospital already in a bad physical, emotional and mental condition. Then if they leave they are physically better (or dead) but spiritually they are worse off than before they went in. The patients lose faith in God and believe the doctor is the one to please, and the way to do that isn't through righteousness, piety or obedience to the divine, but by paying lots of money to the hospital and being "lucky". It seems to me that many hospitals are like casinos, you go inside and it's a gamble whether you'll come out broke physically and financially. Both hospitals and casinos are expensive to stay in and the employees of both places "*wish you luck*" and "*hope you do better*". Yet realistically both casinos and hospitals lose money if those they "service" actually do get better or improve. Both will cost you money and teach you that luck determines success. During my experience in America it's difficult to tell which is more immoral, the casino or the hospital. In the casino they'll try to befriend you as long as you have money, then once you're broke they'll ask you to leave. In the hospital you come in broken and you leave in poverty, financially and spiritually. A person can enter a hospital as an unhealthy believer and then exit as a healthy disbeliever, with "Luck" as their new god. Then visit the casino trying to win money to pay the exorbitant hospital bill or to "enjoy life". Then they return to the hospital to fix physical injuries suffered from not paying their gambling debts. It's the "lucky cycle". The hospitals set em up, the casinos send em back, while Satan watches the show and claps.

Whenever something good happens to a believer they are grateful. Whenever something bad happens to a believer they are patient. In the long term big picture something may seem good in the moment but is bad, and something may seem bad in the moment but is actually good. Either way the believer gets rewarded for displaying gratitude or patience with whatever God decrees.

The disbeliever thinks "luck" is responsible for things, and instead of getting rewarded they are making God angry. Some people actually believe "good luck" will get them into paradise and that "bad luck" will cause them to enter hell. In reality believing in luck of any kind will cause a person to suffer that "unlucky" result of the fire which they fear.

What I'm saying is that God is responsible for the unseen and the unpredicted and "luck" has nothing to do with it. To which maybe you are saying *"Yeah I know, it's just a word okay? Chill out, we don't really believe in "luck"."* Whereas if people don't believe in it they wouldn't use it at all. For instance if you don't believe in Karma you don't go around using the word "Karma" because it's not in your vocabulary. I mention this because of a widespread phenomenon known as a "Pot-Luck" meal. Maybe you've heard of this, maybe you've been to one. Well this has a "lucky" origin, hence the use of the word. Historically the "Pot-luck" dinner has been traced back to 1592 CE when the English playwright Thomas Nashe used the expression in one of his plays, thereby indicating the custom was known to his audience and practiced during, as well as before, that time period. There were various versions that evolved over time, some for individual meals and some for communal, but all of them used the name "Pot-Luck" and were based on the religious belief in "Luck". The term "Pot-Luck" refers to the "luck of the Pot", or chance, or "luck of the draw" in gambling terms in that "luck" determines what you get. Sometimes a parasitic individual, a beggar, or traveler would arrive at one's house unannounced asking for a meal. To be ready for such unexpected occurrences households began to keep something in the cooking pot at all times. Sometimes people would simply keep water in the pot, or frequently put the scraps/leftovers from their meal in the pot to have a soup ready or to flavor the cooking water for the next meal. Then if a unexpected visitor asked for a meal they would be told they'd have a "pot-luck" meal, in that whatever is in the pot at the time they stopped by is what they can have. Occasionally a visitor might have "good Pot-Luck" and stop by while the household was cooking a good wholesome meal, other times it would just be water or leftover scraps. So the "pot-luck" dinner was a form of moocher gambling and was also a way for families to say they fed the poor beggars or their guests without really giving them anything at all. The stingy or cruel person could offer a beggar a "pot-luck" dinner as a joke or way to socially seem charitable without really being charitable, especially if the poor person didn't know what exactly a "pot-luck dinner" meant. While I haven't found any specific recorded instances of this nasty trick occurring, it's easy to speculate that it happened. Over time this joke wouldn't work on the poor anymore and guests realized that eating a household "pot-luck" meal usually tended to be disappointing. Thus the "pot-luck" began to become more of a communal event where people would meet at a public place and everyone would bring a pot to eat from, except they would all have to share together. Thus it was exciting entertainment where none knew what they'd get because it was unknown which pot you would get to eat from. Some would bring real tasty meals and some would bring fake near empty pots, or disgusting meals(as still happens to this day). Thus a "Pot-luck" communal meal involved a great deal of superstition, excitement and dissatisfaction. It was like a game where someone will eat well, someone will barely eat and someone will eat disgusting stuff, and it all depends on the "Pot-luck" or "Luck of the Pots". It became a cheap way to have a communal meal without anybody knowing who the cheap ones were who didn't contribute their fair share. Since gambling was prohibited and frowned upon, this "Pot-luck" was how people gambled socially. Churches couldn't stop it because everyone who brought a pot could participate, so it was excused as a form of charity for the poor who could bring a pot but couldn't afford food to eat/cook. It was basically gambling (and cruelty for some) disguised as anonymous charity, because while a poor person could theoretically get a good meal, they could also end up having to eat something unhealthy, unsanitary and completely disgusting if they didn't have good "pot-luck". Later on the skilled cooks wanted recognition for their superior cooking abilities so it became less secretive as to who brought what. Also as gambling became legalized, gambling with your meal didn't seem as fun. Yet as with gambling, the "Pot-Luck" could be arranged and fixed by the more wealthy/reputable participants and the unfair "Pot-Luck" likely contributed to changes being made to the game. By the 19th century wealthy people decided to lessen their risk and would host "Pot-luck" meals where only first-class cooks would bring a pot to eat from. Other forms of "Pot-Luck" meals involved everyone bringing a pot and pouring their contents into one big pot, basically making a community made soup that was then redistributed to everyone; which again the type of food you got in your soup depended on your "Pot-Luck". Taverns and pubs would perform this type of "Pot-Luck" dinner. This communal semi-equitable "Pot-Luck" was obviously more popular and enjoyable than the cruel gambling type. During the WWII era when food was rationed the masses popularized the tradition of a communal "Pot-Luck" meal. They would meet on a routine basis bringing whatever scraps/leftovers they had collected throughout the week and would all share their weekly leftovers equitably at random, so that by eating the community scraps each week instead of your own in the long run it would result in tastier/more nutritious meals for everyone; that is unless you had bad "Pot-luck". To prevent bad "Pot-luck" certain "Pot-luck clubs" were formed by collective groups who had similar tastes. Therein "Pot-luck" meals changed yet again from being public events to private events. Today it is more similar as to how it was in the middle ages except it's more about gluttony than gambling. Also few dare to bring clearly empty pots or disgusting foods to be cruel/funny and because of the freedom syndrome everyone gets to choose to unsanitarily eat a little from every pot/dish they choose to eat from instead of getting forced to eat just one of the many brought. Whereas while in the past the "Pot-luck" meals were done out of necessity to offer something to an unexpected guest or because of scarce food, with superstition added to give the illusion of it being a good meal, today most are done because of financial stinginess, laziness on behalf of hosts, extravagant culinary competition or as an excuse to get a community to meet together with people whom they probably hate and wouldn't get together with otherwise unless they are treated to a gluttonous feast which will have mystery food served. Thus today it's basically a hyped up dreamy fantasy buffet to entice people to attend thinking it will have the best food the community can collectively concoct, even though in practice it is typically the cheapest buffet the community can concoct where most of the people don't enjoy most of the food. It's popular in democratic countries today because it makes bad cooks seem equal to good cooks since they both get a place in the same line. Unfortunately no qualifications are necessary to bring a dish, nobody asks whether the foods were prepared hygienically or with safe ingredients, they just assume if it's "home-made" it's good. Yet the reason "home-made" food is known as good, is because the cook is known to be safe and sanitary while specially

trying to make something suited to your tastes and dietary uniqueness. "Pot-luck" meals today aren't "home-made" they're made by strangers in places you don't call home who don't know what you like to or can eat, nor do they know what you consider sanitary/edible. In a sense "Pot-luck" meals are like direct democracy for food, in that everyone brings a dish and every dish is eligible for mass consumption. It sounds good in theory but in practice people get sick and it causes community problems and dissatisfaction which is why nobody has "Pot-luck" meals everyday. Although if "Pot-lucks" were representative democracy(as nearly every democratic country in the world claims to be) they'd result in everyone bringing a dish and then everyone being forced to eat what one person chooses to eat with the food selector being decided by majority vote. In reality people prefer to choose what to eat by way of dictatorship and not democracy. I've yet to meet one person who agrees the majority in a restaurant or at a party should vote for one person/cohort who chooses what everyone present will eat. I guess people just value what they put on their plate more than how their government's policies are determined or maybe it's just separation between plate and state.
Nonetheless "Pot-luck" meals today do serve

political purposes of promoting equality despite different quality, teaching that it's the individual's effort that counts and the results they get do not entitle them to any different treatment. Yet that's a whole separate topic of whether merit should be rewarded despite that meaning inequality, but psychologically the "Pot-luck" meals emphasize equality is most important and that merit has no effect on results. That's why the good cooks at a "Pot-luck" end up eating bad food, which to me seems unjust and crazy that someone who cooks a good meal ends up eating a meal of lower quality than that which they made. Even though luck has less of a role in the "Pot-luck" meals of today, it still does play a major role because as everyone knows the good food gets eaten fast and first regardless of who made or brought the good food. The best cook at a "Pot-luck" can even end up at the end of the line and be forced to eat the worst food that was brought or nothing, which is oppression. So by participating in a "Pot-Luck" dinner in modern times one is not only relying on the "Pot-Luck" but also the "Luck of your place in line" as well, which also leads to bribery and cutting in line as well as communal disharmony because few are ever satisfied with the "luck of the line". There is always somebody who's feelings get hurt by getting cut in line, especially when it seriously impacts what they get to eat. Thus these modern "Pot-Luck" dinners promote the religion of "luck" as well as disunity and oppression. Whereas in truth nobody really enjoys them because disgusting food still gets eaten and cooks compete with each other out of envy, sometimes even sabotaging each others foods. Nearly all who participate in "Pot-luck" meals today end up with sore feelings thinking they deserved a better meal based on the time/effort/money spent making the dish/pot they brought. They cause people to blame the community collectively or specific people for their unsatisfied stomach, or the intestinal virus/sickness they get from a bad dish; which leads many to backbite and gossip about the cooks whom they may or may not know. Unfortunately modern frugal gluttonous gamblers' "Pot-luck" dinners end up with more losers than winners. At the very least if the gambling/gluttonous "Pot-luck" meals don't cease, the name "Pot-Luck" should never ever be used. This is because to use the name means to believe in "luck" just as someone who called something a "lucky trinket" indicates a belief in luck, because otherwise they wouldn't use that word to describe their trinket. Thus one cannot have a "Pot-Luck" meal without promoting "Luck". If it had nothing to do with "luck" the word wouldn't be used. So if you use the word "luck" or "lucky" to describe things, you either believe in luck and are promoting it, or don't believe in it but are promoting it which is hypocritical. While in the latter case aside from promoting the concept of "luck" one is also lying through false advertising if they don't believe in "luck". Although it's still false advertising if they believe in "luck", but if they believe in what they're advertising it's a lie by mistake while if they don't believe in the "luck" they're promoting then it's a lie by design. So if you don't believe in "luck" then don't use the word, unless you are denouncing the word/faith explaining why the word "Luck" shouldn't be used to describe things. If "luck" doesn't exist then neither should the word.

In summary "Luck" does not exist, it is a pagan superstition. Truly this idea of "Luck" must be completely eradicated because it is a very dangerous matter that if it's believed in constitutes disbelief in God. Speaking as though luck exists is an offense to God. No matter what your religion is, one who believes in luck cannot possibly believe in God, because such a person has attributed the powers of God to "luck". God did not create luck and no prophet ever endorsed it, it originates straight from the Satanic pagan religions. The disbelieving pagan Babylonian astrologers used to say "good stars" in regards to their hope of goodness for the person because of their pagan belief in horoscopes. When the Jews were exiled to Babylon they picked up this saying as "mazeltov" which subsequently evolved to have the modern non-astrological meaning of "good luck". The belief in "good luck" originates from the ancient pagan belief that "good stars" result in goodness for whoever has "good stars". Luck is basically an expansion of horoscopes. Both of which are pagan beliefs that can cause one to burn in hell forever if they believe in them. Since people couldn't change their zodiac signs and they didn't like being stuck with "bad stars" for life, Satan renovated the zodiac superstition into a more generic less vulnerable version. This is because the zodiac is easier to refute than luck since the zodiac is easy to explain as nonsensical to everyone. For example if you go to another solar system the stars look completely different so basically the zodiac only looks as it does if you are on earth. Thus if one left earth they would have a whole different interpretation of the zodiac and each planet would have a different zodiac tapestry. Therefore the tapestry cannot tell the future or have any meaning for individual humans or events if by changing the angle one is looking at the tapestry it changes the entire picture and subsequent interpretation. The pagans didn't know this because they thought the skies/stars were made special just for the earth and some even thought the sun revolved around the earth because they thought humans were so special, with some even thinking earth was flat which meant their sky would be flat too. Satan also saw a way to industrialize and mass-market disbelief because people could incorporate idols as "good luck" charms, which couldn't be done with the zodiac. Thus people would be more involved in the luck superstition than they would be in the zodiac superstition since there isn't any superstitious thing that one could think of doing to get "good stars". People are more likely to reject a false superstition that says they're doomed from day one. While at the same time belief in "good luck" makes one disbelieve in God's pre-ordainment to a much greater extent than belief in the zodiac does. Although Satan didn't abandon the zodiac trap entirely, some still fall for it while others get lead into it with songs like "*Twinkle Twinkle Little Star*" eventually becoming disbelievers by singing the famous Disney song "*When you wish upon a star*" of which the lyrics plainly contain many statements of disbelief and is actually a prayer for star worship. Yet with Satan spreading the idea of luck he made another road to hell that had more lanes and is easier to travel on, as well as less easily identifiable as a road to hell. I don't want anyone to fall into that "lucky" category of disbelief because of a superstition. Whereas most people who profess not to believe in a god simply make "luck" their god and reason for causes and events. So next time someone wishes you "luck", tell them "*As far as I know Luck does not exist, and there is no evidence to suggest it is anything more than a pagan superstition.*" or you could just ask them if there is any proof that luck exists before explaining the pagan origins luck developed from. To this day no one has ever provided me with proof other than their personal opinion. Every religion that Satan has ever created used personal opinion as its justification. Both the good and bad varieties of "luck" have absolutely no proof to verify their existence and cannot be measured in any way. Though empiricism itself is just as dumb as "luck". It's simple to understand, "Luck" just doesn't exist. There is only 1 definition of Luck which is true.

**Luck:** 1 of the biggest Satanic scams known to man.

Lastly Prophet Muhammad (peace be upon him) said,

*"Taking omens is shirk(associating partners with God); taking omens is shirk. He said it three times. Every one of us has some (superstition), but Allah removes it by trust (in Him)."* Classed as saheeh (authentic) by al-Albaani in Saheeh Abi Dawood.

Al-Bukhaari (5776) and Muslim (2224) narrated from Anas ibn Maalik that the Prophet Muhammad (peace be upon him) said: *"There is no 'adwa (transmission of infectious disease without the permission of Allaah) and no tiyarah (superstitious belief in bad omens), but I like optimism."* They said, *"What is optimism?"* He said, *"A good word."*

Prophet Muhammad pbuh (Musnad Ahmed) also said, *"A person who derived bad luck from something and refrained from doing what he was intending to do, he has committed shirk."* The companions asked him what would be its expiation, the Prophet replied *"He should say,*

اللَّهُمَّ لَا طَيْرَ إِلاَّ طَيْرُكَ وَلاَ خَيْرَ إِلاَّ خَيْرُكَ وَلاَ إِلَهَ غَيْرُكَ.

*' O Allah there is no portent other than Your portent, no goodness other than Your goodness, and none worthy of worship other than You'."*

In closing, to worship includes attributing ultimate causation to something. If ultimate causation is attributed to luck then it has become a rival deity to the true deity of whom none other than the true deity rightly deserves a share of worship. To believe in / trust in something is to worship it.

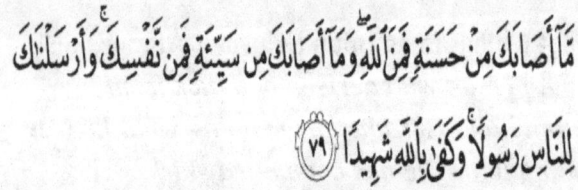

Quran 4:79, *"What comes to you of good is from Allah , but what comes to you of evil,* [O man], *is from yourself.*[due to your sins] *And We have sent you*, [O Muhammad], *to the people as a messenger, and sufficient is Allah as Witness.*